EDWIN MORGAN TWENTIES

TAKE HEART

CELEBRATING EDWIN MORGAN'S CENTENARY

Love
Scotland
Menagerie
Take Heart
Space and Spaces

EDWIN MORGAN TWENTIES

TAKE HEART

SELECTED POEMS

Introduced by
Ali Smith

Polygon

in association with
Carcanet

First published in Great Britain in 2020 by
Polygon, an imprint of Birlinn Ltd, in association with
Carcanet Press Ltd

Birlinn Ltd
West Newington House
10 Newington Road
Edinburgh EH9 1QS

9 8 7 6 5 4 3 2 1

www.polygonbooks.co.uk

ISBN 978 1 84697 545 5

British Library Cataloguing-in-Publication Data
A catalogue record for this book is available
from the British Library.

The publisher gratefully acknowledges investment from
Creative Scotland towards the publication of this book.

Typeset in Verdigris M V B by Polygon, Edinburgh

Printed and bound by Gutenberg, Malta

CONTENTS

INTRODUCTION

This cornucopia of a collection is slim in the hand but full of poems so expansive that as soon as you start to read it the world and its possibilities shift. Its poems are about – about what? Everything: about art and its makings, about forgiveness, kindness, about seemingly impossible renaissance, about the human spirit through time, about the odds stacked against us all, the inevitability of human frailty, the determination of the power-mongerers, the weight and poison of whichever closed religious or political dogma has decided to categorise or lessen us.

Edwin Morgan leans his poetry against the odds and tells himself, and us, in the poem called 'Pelagius' (and in the form of his historical namesake, Morgan, the homegrown ancient theologian of free will who was also known as Pelagius), what to do.

> Morgan, I said to myself, take note,
> Take heart. In a time of confusion
> You must make a stand. There is a chrysalis
> Throbbing to disgorge oppression and pessimism,
> Proscription, prescription, conscription,
> Praying mantises. Cut them down!

A poem about the streetsong of a blind woman reveals an unexpected 'fortitude' and versatility. A poem about a devastating loss of strength pivots on a hard-won 'fierce salvage' in lives wrecked by everyday toughness and fragility, and on the unexpectedly joyous form such salvage takes: 'I learned both love and joy in a hard school.' A poem about the death of Marilyn Monroe reveals the poet's eye – and all our eyes – on the truth versus the fake dream; and the fake dream of religiosity is joyfully excoriated in this collection in poem after poem, moment after moment of sheer liberation, the earthly in its 'pure green glory' telling the angels to get lost and gracing human notions of the spirit with a gorgeous life-love instead.

Perseverance, 'that one persisting patience of the undefeated', as Morgan puts it, unites us, and even if the odds are as ridiculous, as flagrantly hilarious as, say, the task the jigsaw-maker faces in 'From the Video Box 25', the payoff is the kick of real/miraculous transformation that comes with concentrated creativity. This is a discipline that can create worlds out of broken-up pieces, can even sway death, as the speaker does in 'Instructions to an Actor', Morgan's take on Shakespeare's *The Winter's Tale*. Morgan's poetry produces the kind of warmth that thaws winter even though we know full well how cold it is. Look at 'Trio', whose warmth and exclamation are a vision of generosity, from a poet whose work unites generosity and vision, and whose own generosity of vision can renew even cold old, clichéd old Christmas.

This isn't a simple act. In 'The Second Life' he says it: 'A great place and its people are not renewed lightly.' Then he casts his eye round a city waking, a place rebuilding itself out of its own rubble. 'Slip out of darkness,' he says. 'It is time.' He can do that, with time, he can light it, moment to moment, he can fill an ancient Egyptian mummy, stone dead for centuries, with a life and language even more vital than the language time speaks. Morgan's poems argue for the force of a renewal that looks not to the light but to the brightness in light, to the word bright itself shining with lit intelligence, a word etymologically related to the break of day, the everyday rebirth that happens daily wherever we are in life, whatever decade we're in: 'At forty I woke up, saw it was day, / . . . knew Glasgow – what? – knew Glasgow new . . . / And new was no illusion' ('Epilogue: Seven Decades').

His love for Scotland, its 'stubbornness', its 'little bonfires / in cold mist' is another source of this brightness, one which can burn low or high. For instance, in 'Oban Girl', a poem so short and light and self-contained as to seem almost throwaway, he holds a momentary match-flame to a girl caught in time, young and free, and he weighs the split second of her freedom against an inevitable matched future, granting her a kind of immortality in a set of connecting phrases that stop time at the same time as catch its moving beat, the moving beat of her. Whereas in 'Cinquevalli' and 'Vincent Lunardi' he lights the whole sky in poems that celebrate a colourful liberation (and it's no accident the word gay is at the heart of the latter of these bright poems, the last poem in this collection, a word treated with expansiveness, affection, and a lovely, dandified, lighthearted warmth), poems that celebrate lives lived with such a combination of dash, discipline and artistry that in the most human of ways they shake hands with the superhuman. Up against fragility, breakage, shifts of fortune, war? nothing is lost. The flight of a life disciplined to outface the odds; the 'rapture' of human longing met by art, ingenuity and balance, and – what's that at the door? a dying man says. Is it death? 'I am not talking about death!' he says. 'I am talking about life, and life abundant!'

'Forget your literature? – forget your soul.' That's Morgan, in a poem from 2004, called 'Retrieving and Renewing'. Literature and the spirit are ever-related in Edwin Morgan's writing, and this collection in your hands is just a splinter of the flights, the forgiveness, the forward-roll of benign possibility, the skill, the gift and the generosity of a vision and a spirit that says it every time, like Morgan/Pelagius does, refusing to step into his old sarcophagus, standing instead over timeless Glasgow. The world going to chaos, is it ending again? Constraints on the spirit? Dissolve them. Look to our own amazing human grace. Work like prophets, he says. See a future. Now work towards it. Take heart.

Ali Smith

TAKE HEART

BLIND

Almost unconscionably sweet
Is that voice in the city street.
Her fingers skim the leaves of braille.
She sings as if she could not fail
To activate each sullen mind
And make the country of the blind
Unroll among the traffic fumes
With its white stick and lonely rooms.
Even if she had had no words,
Unsentimental as a bird's
Her song would rise in spirals through
The dust and gloom to make it true
That when we see such fortitude,
Though she cannot, the day is good.

Cathures: New Poems 1997–2001
(Carcanet Press/Mariscat Press, 2002)

CINQUEVALLI

Cinquevalli is falling, falling.
The shining trapeze kicks and flirts free,
solo performer at last.
The sawdust puffs up with a thump,
settles on a tangle of broken limbs.
St Petersburg screams and leans.
His pulse flickers with the gas-jets. He lives.

Cinquevalli has a therapy.
In his hospital bed, in his hospital chair
he holds a ball, lightly, lets it roll round his hand,
or grips it tight, gauging its weight and resistance,
begins to balance it, to feel its life attached to his
by will and knowledge, invisible strings
that only he can see. He throws it
from hand to hand, always different,
always the same, always
different, always the
same.
His muscles learn to think, his arms grow very strong.

Cinquevalli in sepia
looks at me from an old postcard: bundle of enigmas.
Half faun, half military man; almond eyes, curly hair,
conventional moustache; tights, and a tunic loaded

with embroideries, tassels, chains, fringes; hand on hip
with a large signet-ring winking at the camera
but a bull neck and shoulders and a cannon-ball
at his elbow as he stands by the posing pedestal;
half reluctant, half truculent,
half handsome, half absurd,
but let me see you forget him: not to be done.

Cinquevalli is a juggler.
In a thousand theatres, in every continent,
he is the best, the greatest. After eight years perfecting
he can balance one billiard ball on another billiard ball
on top of a cue on top of a third billiard ball
in a wine-glass held in his mouth. To those
who say the balls are waxed, or flattened,
he patiently explains the trick will only work
because the spheres are absolutely true.
There is no deception in him. He is true.

Cinquevalli is juggling with a bowler,
a walking-stick, a cigar, and a coin.
Who foresees? How to please.
The last time round, the bowler
flies to his head, the stick sticks in his hand,
the cigar jumps into his mouth, the coin

lands on his foot – ah, but
is kicked into his eye
and held there as the miraculous monocle
without which the portrait would be incomplete.

Cinquevalli is practising.
He sits in his dressing-room talking to some friends,
at the same time writing a letter with one hand
and with the other juggling four balls.
His friends think of demons, but
'You could all do this,' he says,
sealing the letter with a billiard ball.

Cinquevalli is on the high wire in Odessa.
The roof cracks, he is falling, falling
into the audience, a woman breaks his fall,
he cracks her like a flea, but lives.

Cinquevalli broods in his armchair in Brixton Road.
He reads in the paper about the shells whining
at Passchendaele, imagines the mud and the dead.
He goes to the window and wonders through that dark evening
what is happening in Poland where he was born.

His neighbours call him a German spy.
'Kestner, Paul Kestner, that's his name!'
'Keep Kestner out of the British music-hall!'
He frowns; it is cold; his fingers seem stiff and old.

Cinquevalli tosses up a plate of soup
and twirls it on his forefinger; not a drop spills.
He laughs, and well may he laugh
who can do that. The astonished table
breathe again, laugh too, think the world
a spinning thing that spills, for a moment, no drop.

Cinquevalli's coffin sways through Brixton
only a few months before the Armistice.
Like some trick they cannot get off the ground
it seems to burden the shuffling bearers, all their arms
cross-juggle that displaced person, that man
of balance, of strength, of delights and marvels,
in his unsteady box at last into the earth.

Poems of Thirty Years
(Carcanet Press, 1982)

THE COALS

Before my mother's hysterectomy
she cried, and told me she must never bring
coals in from the cellar outside the house,
someone must do it for her. The thing itself
I knew was nothing, it was the thought
of that dependence. Her tears shocked me
like a blow. As once she had been taught,
I was taught self-reliance, discipline,
which is both good and bad. You get things done,
you feel you keep the waste and darkness back
by acts and acts and acts and acts and acts,
bridling if someone tells you this is vain,
learning at last in pain. Hardest of all
is to forgive yourself for things undone,
guilt that can poison life – away with it,
you say, and it is loath to go away.
I learned both love and joy in a hard school
and treasure them like the fierce salvage of
some wreck that has been built to look like stone
and stand, though it did not, a thousand years.

Poems of Thirty Years
(Carcanet Press, 1982)

THE DEATH OF MARILYN MONROE

What innocence? Whose guilt? What eyes? Whose breast?
Crumpled orphan, nembutal bed,
white hearse, Los Angeles,
DiMaggio! Los Angeles! Miller! Los Angeles! America!
That Death should seem the only protector –
That all arms should have faded, and the great cameras and
     lights become an inquisition and a torment –
That the many acquaintances, the autograph-hunters, the
     inflexible directors, the drive-in admirers should become
     a blur of incomprehension and pain –
That lonely Uncertainty should limp up, grinning, with
     bewildering barbiturates, and watch her undress and lie
     down and in her anguish
call for him! call for him to strengthen her with what could
     only dissolve her! A method
of dying, we are shaken, we see it. Strasberg!
Los Angeles! Olivier! Los Angeles! Others die
and yet by this death we are a little shaken, we feel it,
America.
Let no one say communication is a cantword.
They had to lift her hand from the bedside telephone.
But what she had not been able to say
perhaps she had said. 'All I had was my life.

I have no regrets, because if I made
any mistakes, I was responsible.
There is now – and there is the future.
What has happened is behind. So
it follows you around? So what?' – This
to a friend, ten days before.
And so she was responsible.
And if she was not responsible, not wholly responsible,
   Los Angeles? Los Angeles? Will it follow you around?
   Will the slow white hearse of the child of America follow
   you around?

The Second Life
(Edinburgh University Press, 1968)

EPILOGUE: SEVEN DECADES

At ten I read Mayakovsky had died,
learned my first word of Russian, *lyublyu*;
watched my English teacher poke his earwax
with a well-chewed HB and get the class
to join his easy mocking of my essay
where I'd used *verdant herbage* for green grass.
So he was right? So I hated him!
And he was not really right, the ass.
A writer knows what he needs,
as came to pass.

At twenty I got marching orders, kitbag,
farewell to love, not arms (though our sole arms
were stretchers), a freezing Glentress winter
where I was coaxing sticks at six to get
a stove hot for the cooks, found myself picked
quartermaster's clerk – 'this one seems a bit
less gormless than the bloody others' – did
gas drill in the stinging tent, met
Tam McSherry who farted at will
a musical set.

At thirty I thought life had passed me by,
translated *Beowulf* for want of love.
And one night stands in city centre lanes –

they were dark in those days – were wild but bleak.
Sydney Graham in London said 'you know
I always thought so', kissed me on the cheek.
And I translated Rilke's *Loneliness*
is like a rain, and week after week after week
strained to unbind myself,
sweated to speak.

At forty I woke up, saw it was day,
found there was love, heard a new beat, heard Beats,
sent airmail solidarity to São
Paulo's poetic-concrete revolution,
knew Glasgow – what? – knew Glasgow new – somehow –
new with me, with John, with cranes, diffusion
of another concrete revolution, not bad,
not good, but new. And new was no illusion:
a spring of words, a sloughing,
an ablution.

At fifty I began to have bad dreams
of Palestine, and saw bad things to come,
began to write my long unwritten war.

I was a hundred-handed Sindbad then,
rolled and unrolled carpets of blood and love,
raised tents of pain, made the dust into men
and laid the dust with men. I supervised
a thesis on Doughty, that great Englishman
who brought all Arabia back
in his hard pen.

At sixty I was standing by a grave.
The winds of Lanarkshire were loud and high.
I knew what I had lost, what I had had.
The East had schooled me about fate, but still
it was the hardest time, oh more, it was
the worst of times in self-reproach, the will
that failed to act, the mass of good not done.
Forgiveness must be like the springs that fill
deserted furrows if they wait
until – until –

At seventy I thought I had come through,
like parting a bead curtain in Port Said,
to something that was shadowy before,

figures and voices of late times that might
be surprising yet. The beads clash faintly
behind me as I go forward. No candle-light
please, keep that for Europe. Switch the whole thing
right on. When I go in I want it bright,
I want to catch whatever is there
in full sight.

Collected Poems

(Carcanet Press, 1990)

If you ask me what my favourite programme is
it has to be that strange world jigsaw final.
After the winner had defeated all his rivals
with harder and harder jigsaws, he had to prove his mettle
by completing one last absolute mindcrusher
on his own, under the cameras, in less than a week.
We saw, but he did not, what the picture would be:
the mid-Atlantic, photographed from a plane,
as featureless a stretch as could be found,
no weeds, no flotsam, no birds, no oil, no ships,
the surface neither stormy nor calm, but ordinary,
a light wind on a slowly rolling swell.
Hand-cut by a fiendish jigger to simulate,
but not to have, identical beaks and bays,
it seemed impossible; but the candidate –
he said he was a stateless person, called himself Smith –
was impressive: small, dark, nimble, self-contained.
The thousands of little grey tortoises were scattered
on the floor of the studio; we saw the clock; he started.
His food was brought to him, but he hardly ate.
He had a bed, with the light only dimmed to a weird blue,
never out. By the first day he had established
the edges, saw the picture was three metres long
and appeared to represent (dear God!) the sea.
Well, it was a man's life, and the silence

(broken only by sighs, click of wood, plop of coffee
in paper cups) that kept me fascinated.
Even when one hand was picking the edge-pieces
I noticed his other hand was massing sets
of distinguishing ripples or darker cross-hatching or
incipient wave-crests; his mind,
if not his face, worked like a sea.
It was when he suddenly rose from his bed
at two, on the third night, went straight over
to one piece and slotted it into a growing central patch,
then back to bed, that I knew he would make it.
On the sixth day he looked haggard and slow,
with perhaps a hundred pieces left,
of the most dreary unmarked lifeless grey.
The camera showed the clock more frequently.
He roused himself, and in a quickening burst
of activity, with many false starts, began
to press that inhuman insolent remnant together.
He did it, on the evening of the sixth day.
People streamed onto the set. Bands played.
That was fine. But what I liked best
was the last shot of the completed sea,
filling the screen; then the saw-lines disappeared,
till almost imperceptibly the surface moved
and it was again the real Atlantic, glad

to distraction to be released, raised
above itself in growing gusts, allowed
to roar as rain drove down and darkened,
allowed to blot, for a moment, the orderer's hand.

From the Video Box
(Mariscat Press, 1986)

G.M. HOPKINS IN GLASGOW
for J.A.M.R.

Earnestly nervous yet forthright, melted
by bulk and warmth and unimposed rough grace,
he lit a ready fuse from face to face
of Irish Glasgow. Dark tough tight-belted
drunken Fenian poor ex-Ulstermen
crouched round a brazier like a burning bush
and lurched into his soul with such a push
that British angels blanched in mid-amen
to see their soldier stumble like a Red.
Industry's pauperism singed his creed.
He blessed them, frowned, beat on his hands. The load
of coal-black darkness clattering on his head
half-crushed, half-fed the bluely burning need
that trudged him back along the Woodside Road.

Sonnets from Scotland
(Mariscat Press, 1984)

IN THE SNACK-BAR

A cup capsizes along the formica,
slithering with a dull clatter.
A few heads turn in the crowded evening snack-bar.
An old man is trying to get to his feet
from the low round stool fixed to the floor.
Slowly he levers himself up, his hands have no power.
He is up as far as he can get. The dismal hump
looming over him forces his head down.
He stands in his stained beltless gabardine
like a monstrous animal caught in a tent
in some story. He sways slightly,
the face not seen, bent down
in shadow under his cap.
Even on his feet he is staring at the floor
or would be, if he could see.
I notice now his stick, once painted white
but scuffed and muddy, hanging from his right arm.
Long blind, hunchback born, half paralysed
he stands
fumbling with his stick
and speaks:
'I want – to go to the – toilet.'

It is down two flights of stairs, but we go.
I take his arm. 'Give me – your arm – it's better,' he says.
Inch by inch we drift towards the stairs.
A few yards of floor are like a landscape
to be negotiated, in the slow setting out
time has almost stopped. I concentrate
my life to his: crunch of spilt sugar,
slidy puddle from the night's umbrellas,
table edges, people's feet,
hiss of the coffee-machine, voices and laughter,
smell of a cigar, hamburgers, wet coats steaming,
and the slow dangerous inches to the stairs.
I put his right hand on the rail
and take his stick. He clings to me. The stick
is in his left hand, probing the treads.
I guide his arm and tell him the steps.
And slowly we go down. And slowly we go down.
White tiles and mirrors at last. He shambles
uncouth into the clinical gleam.
I set him in position, stand behind him
and wait with his stick.
His brooding reflection darkens the mirror
but the trickle of his water is thin and slow,
an old man's apology for living.
Painful ages to close his trousers and coat –

I do up the last buttons for him.
He asks doubtfully, 'Can I – wash my hands?'
I fill the basin, clasp his soft fingers round the soap.
He washes, feebly, patiently. There is no towel.
I press the pedal of the drier, draw his hands
gently into the roar of the hot air.
But he cannot rub them together,
drags out a handkerchief to finish.
He is glad to leave the contraption, and face the stairs.
He climbs, and steadily enough.
He climbs, we climb. He climbs
with many pauses but with that one
persisting patience of the undefeated
which is the nature of man when all is said.
And slowly we go up. And slowly we go up.
The faltering, unfaltering steps
take him at last to the door
across that endless, yet not endless waste of floor.
I watch him helped on a bus. He shudders off in the rain.
The conductor bends to hear where he wants to go.

Wherever he could go it would be dark
and yet he must trust men.
Without embarrassment or shame
he must announce his most pitiful needs

in a public place. No one sees his face.
Does he know how frightening he is in his strangeness
under his mountainous coat, his hands like wet leaves
stuck to the half-white stick?
His life depends on many who would evade him.
But he cannot reckon up the chances,
having one thing to do,
to haul his blind hump through these rains of August.
Dear Christ, to be born for this!

The Second Life
(Edinburgh University Press, 1968)

INSTRUCTIONS TO AN ACTOR

Now, boy, remember this is the great scene.
You'll stand on a pedestal behind a curtain,
the curtain will be drawn, and then you don't move
for eighty lines; don't move, don't speak, don't breathe.
I'll stun them all out there, I'll scare them,
make them weep, but it depends on you.
I warn you eighty lines is a long time,
but you don't breathe, you're dead,
you're a dead queen, a statue,
you're dead as stone, new-carved,
new-painted and the paint not dry
– we'll get some red to keep your lips shining –
and you're a mature woman, you've got dignity,
some beauty still in middle age, and
you're kind and true, but you're dead,
your husband thinks you're dead,
the audience thinks you're dead,
and you don't breathe, boy, I say
you don't even blink for eighty lines,
if you blink you're out!
Fix your eye on something and keep watching it.
Practise when you get home. It can be done.
And you move at last – music's the cue.
When you hear a mysterious solemn jangle
of instruments, make yourself ready.

Five lines more, you can lift a hand.
It may tingle a bit, but lift it –
slow, slow –
O this is where I hit them
right between the eyes, I've got them now –
I'm making the dead walk –
you move a foot, slow, steady, down,
you guard your balance in case you're stiff,
you move, you step down, down from the pedestal,
control your skirt with one hand, the other hand
you now hold out –
O this will melt their hearts if nothing does –
to your husband who wronged you long ago
and hesitates in amazement
to believe you are alive.
Finally he embraces you, and there's nothing
I can give you to say, boy,
but you must show that you have forgiven him.
Forgiveness, that's the thing. It's like a second life.
I know you can do it. – Right then, shall we try?

Poems of Thirty Years
(Carcanet Press, 1982)

JACK LONDON IN HEAVEN

Part the clouds, let me look down.
Oh god that earth. A breeze comes from the sea
and humpback fogs blanch off to blindness, the sun
hits Frisco, it shines solid up to heaven.
I can't bear not to see brisk day on the Bay,
it drives me out of my mind but I can't bear
not to watch the choppy waters, Israfel.
I got a sea-eagle once to come up here
screaming and turn a prayer-wheel or two
with angry buffets till the sharpshooters
sent him to hell, and I groaned,
grew dark with disfavour. – What,
I should pray now? For these thoughts?
Here are some more. I was up at four
for psalms, shawms, smarms, salaams, yessirs, yesmaams,
felt-tipped hosannas melting into mist,
a mushroom high, an elation of vapours,
a downpour of dumpy amens. Azazel,
I am sick of fireflies. It's a dumb joss.
– You know I'm a spoilt angel? What happens to us?
I'm not so bright – or bright, perhaps. God knows!
They almost let me fall through heaven craning
to see sunshine dappling the heaving gunmetal
of the Oakland Estuary – the crawl, the swell, the crests
I could pull up to touch and wet my hands

let down a moment into time and space.
How long will they allow me to remember
as I pick the cloud-rack apart and peer?
The estuary, Israfel, the glittery estuary, August '96!
My last examination has scratched to a finish,
I'm rushing to the door, whooping and squawking,
I dance down the steps, throw my hat in the air
as the dusty invigilator frowns, gathers in
that furious harvest of four months' cramming,
nineteen hours a day – my vigils, Azazel,
my holy vigils – the oyster-pirate hammering
at the gates of the state university.
It's enough. I got in. But at that time
I took a boat out on the ebb
to be alone where no book ever was.
I scudded dreaming through the creamy rings
of light and water, followed the shore
and thought of earth and heaven and myself
till I saw a shipyard I knew, and the delta rushes
and the weeds and the tin wharves, and smelt the ropes
and some tobacco-smoke, and longed for company.
 – Evensong? I'm not coming to evensong.
Get off, get away. Go on, sing for your supper!
Bloody angels! – So I sailed in, made fast,
and there was Charley, and Liz, and Billy and Joe, and Dutch

– that desperate handsome godlike drunken man –
old friends, Azazel, old friends that clambered over me
and sang and wept and filled me with whisky and beer
brought teetering across the railroad tracks
all that long noon.
They would have kept me there, oh, for ever
but I could see the blue through the open door,
that blue, my sea, and they knew
I had to be away, and got me stumbling down the wharf steps
into a good salmon boat, with charcoal and a brazier
and coffee and a pot and a pan and a fresh-caught fish
and cast me off into a stiff wind.
I tell you, Israfel, the sea was white
and half of it was in my boat
with my sail set hard like a board.
Everything whipped and cracked
in pure green glory as
I stood braced at the mast
and roared out 'Shenandoah'.
Did Odysseus get to heaven?
I came down to earth, at Antioch,
sobered in the sunset shadows, tied up
alongside a potato sloop, had friends
aboard there too, who sizzled my fish for me
and gave me stew and crusty bread and claret,

claret in great pint mugs, and wrapped me in blankets
warmer and softer than the clouds of heaven.
What did we not talk of as we smoked,
sea-tales Odysseus might have known,
under the same night wind, the same wild rigging.
– Azazel, I must get down there!
I am a wasting shade, I am drifting and dying
by these creeping streams. If you are my friend,
tell them my trouble. Tell them
they cannot make me a heaven
like the tide-race and the tiller
and a broken-nailed hand
and the shrouds of Frisco.

Poems of Thirty Years
(Carcanet Press, 1982)

THE MUMMY

(The Mummy [of Rameses II] *was met at Orly airport by Mme Saunier-Seïté.*

> – News item, Sept. 1976)

– May I welcome Your Majesty to Paris.

– Mm.

– I hope the flight from Cairo was reasonable.

– Mmmmm.

– We have a germ-proof room at the Museum of Man
   where we trust Your Majesty will have peace and quiet.

– Unh-unh.

– I am sorry, but this is necessary.
   Your Majesty's person harbours a fungus.

– Fng fng's, hn?

– Well, it is something attacking your cells.
  Your Majesty is gently deteriorating
  after nearly four thousand years
  becalmed in masterly embalmment.
  We wish to save you from the worm.

– Wrm hrm! Mgh-mgh-mgh.

– Indeed I know it must be distressing
  to a pharaoh and a son of Ra,
  to the excavator of Abu Simbel
  that glorious temple in the rock,
  to the perfecter of Karnak hall,
  to the hammer of the Hittites,
  to the colossus whose colossus
  raised in red granite at holy Thebes
  sixteen-men-high astounds the desert
  shattered, as Your Majesty in life
  shattered the kingdom and oppressed the poor
  with such lavish grandeur and panache,
  to Rameses, to Ozymandias,
  to the Louis Quatorze of the Nile,
  how bitter it must be to feel

a microbe eat your camphored bands.
But we are here to help Your Majesty.
We shall encourage you to unwind.
You have many useful years ahead.

– M' n'm 'zym'ndias, kng'v kngz!

– Yes yes. Well, Shelley is dead now.
He was not embalmed. He will not write
about Your Majesty again.

– T't'nkh'm'n? H'tsh'ps't?
'khn't'n? N'f'rt'ti? Mm? Mm?

– The hall of fame has many mansions.
Your Majesty may rest assured
your deeds will always be remembered.

– Youmm w'm'nn. B't'f'lll w'm'nnnn.
No w'm'nnn f'r th'zndz y'rz.

– Your Majesty, what are you doing?

– Ng! Mm. Mhm. Mm? Mm? Mmmmm.

– Your Majesty, Your Majesty! You'll break your stitches!

– Fng st'chez fng's wrm hrm.

– I really hate to have to use
  a hypodermic on a mummy,
  but we cannot have you strain yourself.
  Remember your fungus, Your Majesty.

– Fng. Zzzzzzzz.

– That's right.

– Aaaaaaaaah.

Poems of Thirty Years
(Carcanet Press, 1982)

OBAN GIRL

A girl in a window eating a melon
eating a melon and painting a picture
painting a picture and humming Hey Jude
humming Hey Jude as the light was fading

In the autumn she'll be married

Twelve Songs
(The Castlelaw Press, 1970)

AN OLD WOMAN'S BIRTHDAY

That's me ninety-four. If we are celebrating
I'll take a large Drambuie, many thanks,
and then I'll have a small one every evening
for the next six years. After that – something quick
and I'll be off. A second century doesn't entice.
When I was a girl, you thought you would live for ever.
Those endless summer twilights under the trees,
sauntering, talking, clutching a modest glass
of grampa's punch diluted to suit young ladies –
diluted? It didn't seem so! The crafty old man
loved to see us glowing, certainly not swaying
but just ever so slightly, what do you say, high.

Life put all that away. I drove an ambulance
through shells, ruins, mines, cries, blood,
frightful, days of frightfulness who could forget?

It is not to be dwelt on; we do what we can.
If this is hell, and there is no other,
we are tempered, I was tempered – fires, fires –
I was a woman then, I was not broken.
No angel either; the man I married knew that!
Well, we had our times. What are quarrels for
but to make amends, get stronger. We did, we were.
He is gone now. I don't have a budgie in a cage

but I am one, and if you want me to sing
it will take more than cuttlebone and mirror:
more than Drambuie: more than if there was ever
good news out of Iraq where my ambulance
would keep me day and night without sleep:
more than what I say here, sitting
waiting for my son to come and see me
perhaps with flowers, chocolate, a card,
oh I don't know, he is late, he is ill,
he is old, I forget his heart is worse
than mine, but still, I know he'll do his best.

You really want me to sing? Come on then,
you sing first, then a duet, I love a duet.

A Book of Lives
(Carcanet Press, 2007)

PELAGIUS

I, Morgan, whom the Romans call Pelagius,
Am back in my own place, my green Cathures
By the frisky firth of salmon, by the open sea
Not far, place of my name, at the end of things
As it must seem. But it is not a dream
Those voyages, my hair grew white at the tiller,
I have been where I say I have been,
And my cheek still burns for the world.
That sarcophagus by the Molendinar –
Keep the lid on, I am not stepping into it yet!
I used to think of the grey rain and the clouds
From my hot cave in the Negev, I shooed
The scuttle of scorpions. I had a hat –
You should have seen me – against the sun
At its zenith in that angry Palestine.
I spoke; I had crowds; there was a demon in me.
There had been crowds four centuries before,
And what had come of that? That was the question.
I did not keep back what I had to say.
Some were alarmed. They did not like my red hair.
But I had a corps of friends who shouldered
Every disfavour aside, took ship with me
Westward over the heaving central sea.
We came to Carthage then, and not alone.
The city was seething livid with refugees.

Such scenes, such languages! Such language!
The Goths were in Rome. I saw a master
I had studied under, wild-eyed,
Clutching tattered scrolls, running.
I saw a drift of actors with baskets
Brimming broken masks, they gestured
Bewildered beyond any mime.
I saw a gladiator with half a sword.
I heard a Berber's fiddle twang like the end of a world.
Morgan, I said to myself, take note,
Take heart. In a time of confusion
You must make a stand. There is a chrysalis
Throbbing to disgorge oppression and pessimism,
Proscription, prescription, conscription,
Praying mantises. Cut them down!

One stood against me:
Distinguished turncoat, ex-Manichee, ex this and that,
Preacher of chastity with a son in tow,
A Christian pistoned by new-found fervour,
Born of the desert sand in occupied land,
Bishop in Hippo brandishing anathemas,
Bristling with intelligence not my intelligence,
Black-hearted but indefatigable –
Augustine! You know who you are
And I know who you are and we shall die

Coeval as we came to life coeval.
We are old. The dark is not far off.
It is four hundred years now since those nails
Were hammered in that split the world
And not just flesh. Text and anti-text
Crush the light. You can win,
Will win, I can see that, crowd me out
With power of councils, but me –
Do you know me, can you believe
I have something you cannot have –
My city, not the city of God –
It is to come, and why, do you know why?

Because no one will believe without a splash from a font
Their baby will howl in eternal cold, or fire,
And no one will suffer the elect without merit
To lord it over a cringing flock, and no one
Is doomed by Adam's sin to sin for ever,
And who says Adam's action was a sin,
Or Eve's, when they let history in.

Sometimes when I stand on Blythswood Hill
And strain my eyes (they are old now) to catch
Those changing lights of evening, and the clouds
Going their fiery way towards the firth,
I think we must just be ourselves at last
And wait like prophets – no, not wait, work! –
As prophets do, to see the props dissolve,
The crutches, threats, vain promises,
Altars, ordinances, comminations
Melt off into forgetfulness.
My robe flaps; a gull swoops; man is all.
Cathurian towers will ring this hill.
Engines unheard of yet will walk the Clyde.
I do not even need to raise my arms,
My blessing breathes with the earth.
It is for the unborn, to accomplish their will
With amazing, but only human, grace.

Cathures: New Poems 1997–2001
(Carcanet Press/Mariscat Press, 2002)

PILATE AT FORTINGALL

A Latin harsh with Aramaicisms
poured from his lips incessantly; it made
no sense, for surely he was mad. The glade
of birches shamed his rags, in paroxysms
he stumbled, toga'd, furred, blear, brittle, grey.
They told us he sat here beneath the yew
even in downpours; ate dog-scraps. Crows flew
from prehistoric stone to stone all day.
'See him now.' He crawled to the cattle-trough
at dusk, jumbled the water till it sloshed
and spilled into the hoof-mush in blue strands,
slapped with useless despair each sodden cuff,
and washed his hands, and watched his hands, and washed
his hands, and watched his hands, and washed his hands.

Sonnets from Scotland
(Mariscat Press, 1984)

THE SECOND LIFE

But does every man feel like this at forty –
I mean it's like Thomas Wolfe's New York, his
heady light, the stunning plunging canyons, beauty –
pale stars winking hazy downtown quitting-time,
and the winter moon flooding the skyscrapers, northern –
an aspiring place, glory of the bridges, foghorns
are enormous messages, a looming mastery
that lays its hand on the young man's bowels
until he feels in that air, that rising spirit
all things are possible, he rises with it
until he feels that he can never die –
Can it be like this, and is this what it means
in Glasgow now, writing as the aircraft roar
over building sites, in this warm west light
by the daffodil banks that were never so crowded and lavish –
green May, and the slow great blocks rising
under yellow tower cranes, concrete and glass and steel
out of a dour rubble it was and barefoot children gone –
Is it only the slow stirring, a city's renewed life
that stirs me, could it stir me so deeply
as May, but could May have stirred
what I feel of desire and strength
like an arm saluting a sun?

All January, all February the skaters
enjoyed Binghams's pond, the crisp cold evenings,
they swung and flashed among car headlights,
the drivers parked round the unlit pond
to watch them, and give them light, what laughter
and pleasure rose in the rare lulls
of the yards-away stream of wheels along Great Western Road!
The ice broke up, but the boats came out.
The painted boats are ready for pleasure.
The long light needs no headlamps.

Black oar cuts a glitter: it is heaven on earth.

Is it true that we come alive
not once, but many times?
We are drawn back to the image
of the seed in darkness, or the greying skin
of the snake that hides a shining one –
it will push that used-up matter off
and even the film of the eye is sloughed –
That the world may be the same, and we are not
and so the world is not the same,
the second eye is making again

this place, these waters and these towers,
they are rising again
as the eye stands up to the sun,
as the eye salutes the sun.

Many things are unspoken
in the life of a man, and with a place
there is an unspoken love also
in undercurrents, drifting, waiting its time.
A great place and its people are not renewed lightly.
The caked layers of grime
grow warm, like homely coats.
But yet they will be dislodged
and men will still be warm.
The old coats are discarded.
The old ice is loosed.
The old seeds are awake.

Slip out of darkness, it is time.

The Second Life
(Edinburgh University Press, 1968)

TO IAN HAMILTON FINLAY

Maker of boats,
earthships,
the white cradle
with its patchwork quilt,
toys of wood
painted bright as
the zebras' music
in your carousel,
patiently cut
space cleanly!
There's dark earth
underneath, not far
the North Sea,
a beach goes out
greyer than Dover's
for ignorant armies.
Scotland is
the little bonfires
in cold mist,
with stubbornness,
the woman knits
late by a window,
a man repairing
nets, a man carv-
ing steady glass,

hears the world,
bends to his work.
You give the pleasure
of made things,
the construction holds
like a net, or it
unfolds in waves
a certain measure,
of affection.
Native, familiar as
apples, tugs,
girls, letters from
your moulin,
but
drinking tea
you set for Albers
his saucer of milk.

The Second Life
(Edinburgh University Press, 1968)

TRIO

Coming up Buchanan Street, quickly, on a sharp winter
    evening
a young man and two girls, under the Christmas lights –
The young man carries a new guitar in his arms,
the girl on the inside carries a very young baby,
and the girl on the outside carries a Chihuahua.
And the three of them are laughing, their breath rises
in a cloud of happiness, and as they pass
the boy says, 'Wait till he sees this but!'
The Chihuahua has a tiny Royal Stewart tartan coat like a
    teapot-holder,
the baby in its white shawl is all bright eyes and mouth like
    favours in a fresh sweet cake,
the guitar swells out under its milky plastic cover, tied at the
    neck with silver tinsel tape and a brisk sprig of mistletoe.
Orphean sprig! Melting baby! Warm Chihuahua!
The vale of tears is powerless before you.
Whether Christ is born, or is not born, you
put paid to fate, it abdicates

                    under the Christmas lights.

Monsters of the year,
go blank, are scattered back,
can't bear this march of three.

– And the three have passed, vanished in the crowd
(yet not vanished, for in their arms they wind
the life of men and beasts, and music,
laughter ringing them round like a guard)
at the end of this winter's day.

The Second Life
(Edinburgh University Press, 1968)

AUNT MYRA (1901–1989)

A horse in a field in a picture is easy.
A man in a room with a fan, we wonder.
It might be whirring blades in steamy downtown –
but no, it's what she's left beside her dance-cards.
How she sat out a foxtrot at the Plaza
and fanned her brow, those far-off flirty Twenties
he opens and shuts with an unpractised gesture
that leaves the years half-laughing at the pathos
of the clumsy, until rising strings have swept them
dancing again into silence. The room darkens
with a blue lingering glow above the roof-tops
but the man still stands there, holding up the dangling
dance-cards by their tiny attached pencils.
The cords which are so light seem to him heavy
as if they were about to take the strain of
tender evenings descending into memory.
Something is hard, not easy, though it's clearly
a man, a fan, a woman, a room, a picture.

Hold Hands among the Atoms
(Mariscat Press, 1991)

VINCENT LUNARDI

I do not know what is wrong with me.
I am sick, I lie like lead on this bed.
The sisters took me in. I hear their bells
And the dull rumour of Lisbon beyond these walls.
I am so poor I have nothing.
I have nothing and I am nothing.
The world has shrunk to a bowl of gruel
When the sun goes down. Another world
Is not yet closed, my memories.
I summon them and they come running.
Why can I not rise to greet them?
To rise was my life, I was born for it!

I still remember that early dream of flight.
Playing in the olive groves of Lucca
I stretched my arms to match the dragonflies,
Buzzed and zigzagged like a bee, but most,
Oh most and best, I watched the summer swallow
Slicing the air with a rapture I gave to it
From my own longing. I would have the air,
I would have it someday!
                              Twenty years ago
The air was indeed mine, I was an aeronaut –
I was not the first, I don't claim that, but
I was noted, I was marked, I was famous,

I was loved, I was honoured, I was feted
In England and Scotland, Italy and Spain,
Even in dusty Portugal where I am dying.
But I am not talking about death!
I am talking about life and life abundant!
I have enough breath to spell it.
Memory breaks the sound barrier.
We are off and away, back to happy Glasgow
Where I rose twice from the dead
Tussocks of Glasgow Green and made a wonder.
The hydrogen roared, the flaccid silk blossomed
To a great pod of pink and yellow and green
Stretched taut and shimmering into the blue.
I leapt into the decorated basket,
Decorative myself if I may say so,
Dressed in my regimental colours –
Neapolitan if you want to know –
With a good leg, many ladies commend it,
Waving my flag and blowing my speaking-trumpet
While a band blared the most rousing of marches,
Bells were pealed, and the people waved

To my waving, and exclaimed and shouted and whistled
From tens of thousands of upturned faces
As my six-men-high balloon majestically
Lifted above that ever-living city.
Do you think I cut a figure, cut a dash
In that airy cabin, in my stockings of silk,
My lacy cuffs, my goffered cravat, my – ah,
That hat! – was I not gay that day
And was it not the gayest of days?
The ladies thought so: some clapped, some fainted,
All had eyes for the aeronaut. Do you know
Some of them later helped me to patch
A rent in the balloon, and I gave them
A thread or two of silk: some said
It would become a locket in their bosoms.
Why do I say these things? I had no lady.
I danced a minuet, kissed here and there.
But my only bride was the high air.

I wonder who will remember Lunardi
That soared among the clouds and saw below him
Trongate and Tontine, and the Saracen's Head

Where he lodged and talked the night into pleasure?
It is like a dream of the gay times
That are possible and to be so cherished
We have a little comfort to be taken
As the shadows close in. They do, they do.
It is cold too. Who is that standing in the door?

Cathures: New Poems 1997–2001

(Carcanet Press/Mariscat Press, 2002)

ABOUT THE AUTHOR

EDWIN MORGAN (1920–2010) was born in Glasgow, and spent his life there except for his six years with the Royal Army Medical Corps in the Middle East. He studied English Literature at the University of Glasgow, where he went on to teach, retiring as Professor Emeritus in 1980. He was appointed Glasgow's Poet Laureate in 1999, and awarded the Queen's Gold Medal for Poetry in 2000. In 2004 he was appointed the first Scots Makar of modern times, and wrote the poem 'For the Opening of the Scottish Parliament' in the same year. His poetry is praised for its linguistic inventiveness, social realism and humane curiosity. He wrote concrete and visual poetry, opera libretti and collaborated with jazz saxophonist Tommy Smith to set his work to music; he was also a translator, playwright and critic. Morgan's work is renowned for its outward-looking internationalism, his poetic gaze moving from Europe to the wider world and into space, yet always returning to Glasgow, whose people and landscape he so memorably evoked and imagined.